Overwintering

PIPPA LITTLE was born in East Africa and raised in Scotland. She now lives in Northumberland with her husband, sons and dog. She has worked in editing, literacy and higher education and was awarded a doctorate in contemporary women's poetry from the University of London. Her first collection, *The Spar Box* (2006), was a Poetry Book Society Pamphlet Choice. She has been the winner of an Eric Gregory Award, the Biscuit International Poetry Prize, the Norman MacCaig Centenary Prize, the Andrew Waterhouse Northern Promise Award and the Scotsman Haiku Prize.

T0164283

Also available from Oxford*Poets* / Carcanet Press

PIPPA LITTLE

Overwintering

Oxford*Poets*

CARCANET

First published in Great Britain in 2012 by
Carcanet Press Limited
Alliance House
Cross Street
Manchester M2 7AQ

www.carcanet.co.uk

A CIP catalogue record for this book is available from the British Library

ISBN 978 1 906188 06 1

The publisher acknowledges financial assistance from the Arts Council of England

Typeset by XL Publishing Services, Tiverton
Printed and bound in England by SRP Ltd, Exeter

for Jack, Theo and Sam with love

Acknowledgements

'This Was the Year', 'The Flowering', 'The Captain Plays Shostakovitch…', 'Beijing Flight, Thursday Morning', 'Stella Maris', 'Night-Flying Bees', 'Newala' and 'Spending One Day with Patrick Kavanagh' were all in *Oxford Poets 2010: An Anthology*, edited by David Constantine, Robyn Marsack and Bernard O'Donoghue (Carcanet Press, 2010).

'My Autopsy' was Commended in the Coffee-House Poetry / Troubadour Prize 2008.

'Still Life' was Commended in the Wigtown Book Festival Poetry Competition 2011.

'Bellefield Avenue' was published as 'Home' in *The Snow Globe* (Red Squirrel Press, 2011).

'Our Lady of the Snows' and 'In the City of the Headless Overcoat' were first published in *The Spar Box* (Vane Women Press, 2006).

'Night-Flying Bees' was the winner of the 2007 Myths and Legends Writing competition, Lit and Phil Library, Newcastle.

'This Was the Year' was the winner of the 2009 Biscuit International Poetry Prize.

'Clown Wife' was published online at *ink sweat and tears*, edited by Helen Ivory (www.inksweatandtears.co.uk).

'Mrs Greathead's Garden' was the Diamond Twig Press Poem of the Month for May 2009 (www.diamondtwig.co.uk).

'Simrishamn' won second prize in the Virginia Warbey Poetry Competition 2009.

'Elspeth Owen's bowl' was included in *Soul Feathers: An Anthology for MacMillans* (Indigo Dreams, 2010).

'Coalend Hill Farm 1962' won the Norman MacCaig Centenary Poetry Prize 2010 and has appeared in *Northwords Now* (www.northwordsnow.co.uk) and *Best British Poetry 2011*, edited by Roddy Lumsden (Salt Publishing, 2011). It was also chosen as one of the twenty Best Scottish Poems of 2011, and featured on the Scottish Poetry Library website.

Other poems have been published in *Antiphon*, *Dreamcatcher*, *The Interpreter's House*, *Magma*, *North*, *Obsessed with Pipework*, *Orbis*, *Other Poetry*, *Poetry Salzburg Review*, *Scintilla*.

With thanks to Gillian Allnutt, Paul Batchelor, Sean O'Brien, David Constantine and Judith Willson, as always to Bob Little, all from my writing groups and workshops and to Christina Blackwell.

Contents

Solstice

The shortest day:
dusk falls like a stone to earth.

Yellow, with greenness of lemons in it.
Carpet of snow the long night,

a lopped pelt, dog or wolf.
Yet, light in unexpected places.

I have come through.

My house, a traveller returned,
baring the small, lit window of its heart.

In-gathering of holly, conifer,
red berries for birds' beaks.

Mistletoe and kindling,
incense of forests,

these mists, floating among us.

Span

By what agreement did I spend those years
holding still the shallows of that furred glass tank
so no wilful flurry might trouble your stone-lidded eyes?

One week to the day before you died
a sparrowhawk crashed the window where you sat,
burned plane corkscrewing out of blue sky into a blind wall

just to outstare you:

we said he came to take you on your journey,
for since then, thaws have washed away your home
and way down-river

is where I dream you now,
wild gleam of fin
a fiery wing –

I cup my hands.
March snow wants to be clouds
crossing to the west, forming

and re-forming continents too fragile for occupation:
the clouds want to be horses, only
so far and no further,

not to the world's edge.
I see how, even if I wanted to, I couldn't stay
one span of a heartbeat longer

yet my palms are full,
are full and running over.

Axis

Lying in his last bed
my father remembers his feet
far down in the dark, lost
like a ticket:

cold and soft untouchables
they are forgetting about shoes,
about the metallic lips of stairs,
the earth's axis.

I Meet You Coming Home

The halls of the living are empty,
their long doors locked
their mirrors shrouded
but some lamps have been left burning.

Down on North Street, bright sharps of rain
embed in your shoulders: between us,
every second,
dark matter is pouring

through my body, your body, through
brick walls and walled-up windows,
flat starfields
pricked by eternity:

you keep on coming
as you always did, like Felix,
like Kierkegaard, walking,
you walk right through me, and keep going.

Windfall

A death
that hadn't had its own life yet.

Nothing to show
how something was started
and began to work,
beating towards us.

My hand fits around its hard head
waiting for a face.

Cairn

The first hour was difficult.
The field very soft,
the beginning always slow,
cleaving each block along its grain.

The beginning always slow,
light on the wet, deep stone
beginning to have a presence:
guardian or sentinel to the village

my children will grow up with.
Today the work was slow.
I try to keep my nerve. This is the belly,
this is my home,

where I am most exposed.
I remember the stones on the hill:
still feel them in my hands,
the lifting, cutting, placing.

With things taken away from the land
and things given to it,
part of me stays with the stone,
part of the stone stays with me.

After Flooding

Wood

Many are down:
some far gone, others new-fallen,

leggy, dismembered.
We pick a way around them,

one, overcome, unwinds
silver wrappings from a red wound

that at the press of my finger
coughs puffball dust;

brought down like a hunted beast,
swooned into the ground she loves now

more than any sky, or memory of flying.

Rabbit

Today we hacked clarts and outlaw grass with a blunted spade
to rough a space, brick-sized, out of the earth.

Lifted
he was long as a human child newborn

clutched upside down by the ankles
before we tucked him in.

Home News

Primroses and violets seen on the common,
sadly, mid-morning, the rain came on:
Beatlemania hit the East Hall on Saturday night.

Litter blown eastwards from Lower Main Street.
Caravans to rent, no children, pets or DSS,
Witches' Tours – All Year Round.

Spiders crawl out of relegation zone,
Hamburg Spangle, First At Show.
Concern after sewage enters Eden.

Roll up to Kingdom Carpets!
Peacefully, after a long illness.
And when did you last visit us?

River Walking to the Hermitage

She is not walking in these deeps,
only dreaming them. Such a narrow way,
constant but unsteady. She loops
through amber, weed-spattered
cold washing clean her thighs.

The river turns on cliffs soft-stretched as vellum.
If she keeps dreaming she can reach his cell,
its altar stone a cup
sipping blessings from the ceiling,
where he lived quiet,
rowed a homemade boat,
prayed and watched for weather,

her body a series of points
along the way, neither ferryman nor bell's ring
but a bridge she may choose to cross
or not,
a borealis smudge on the angle of his iris.

My Autopsy

Disintegrate me gently: I am slices of pink-skin sushi,
slides of eyelash and lipstick, sand from under my thumbnail, a faint
smudge of that sandalwood you hated:

swab my throat, flash my bones, unzip
the two curls of my red-sea ribcage, weigh my heart,
my lights, my liver in your metal bowl,

separate the grains and sinews of my last meal, last smile, last
kiss, peel me like a peach, slightly over-ripe, split my
old rose layers of tissue from their yellowed sleeves:

your long gaze sweeps me the way sea searches shingle
all along the beach. Or how the lighthouse
seeped its blue light between our curtains.

I am clean now. Blank as a runway, an unloading ramp.
I have tried to tell you, I have tried so hard to tell you
there was a house you wandered through

leaving your prints on the door, your breath on the downstairs
                                                        window,
not noticing the flowers there, the lilies, or the books
in languages you never learned.

This Was the Year

This was the year before the year
that collapsed on us, a roof brought down by snow.
The year of riding through abandoned stations
on the riverside line that never crossed the river
but danced among warehouses, silos and factories (deceased)
beside battleships settling into red mud.
This was the year that, too exhausted to sleep,
I boiled down the pink and ivory and blue of other women's hands
into a single grey slab. The soap pot next the soup,
fumes of gardenia and bone.
This was the year we were always coming home.
Three steps and a garden where the splayed trike in the frost said
better to have careless love than none at all.
This was the year before the year
I found out that we are fused from lightning, our bodies
maps across which electrical storms flare
and move on. This was the year
extremely far rooftops and lit windows
seen from a plane flying its late night mission
had their glow zapped by pinball fire.
This was the year I closed the door underneath the porch light
and stood out on the first of the three front steps, listening.
Our children's beds expecting their bodies
to come warm them like small fires
but growing cold with waiting.

Half Moon One-Legged Man

October rain on red leaves. He
won't go by the road where the rooks flap, burning,
but lopes through the woods on his one leg,

swinging like a gold watch:
his spoor, punched out, could be blind eyes
filling with tears: they'd say
a god stopped here, and drank.

Still Life

for Louise Hislop

You found a bee
cold-stunned
in garden grass

and sliding your left hand under,
cupped it like a brooch,
thought you'd like it for the microscope.

It lay on your skin
as if upon clouds
summoned by its Maker

but then shuddered
in the bowl of your hand,
exhausted, alive:

you opened your mouth
close above
and blew –

till slowly it began
to twitch, uncurl,
puff out its dandelion fur,

coming back
on your out-breath,
to a damp nest, world

it could leave now,
lifting into morning
without looking back.

Dew Point

Midwinter:
evening begins by 2 pm,
soon moves inwards. You are not
coming home. I push down the lid of your piano,
still warm, don't watch for frost but out there it begins anyway,
running the cracks, pressing up against our walls as the ground grows colder.
You wrote: *I damage everyone who loves me.*
Borne by sub-freezing air, breath transmutes
to ice; how snow and cloud, or you and I
might meet, touch briefly,
delicate as seahorses,
unicorns.

The Flowering

We dig with our sore hands in cold midsummer.
The map reference, four hours by helicopter from any habitation.
An eagle crosses us and turns. The sky's glass,
the wind's hungry. There's nobody I love
    within a day or night of here.

No-man's-land of four converging countries.
Barbed wire, mounds of stone.
The souls of the Pazyryk observe us,
random flies, muddling down
    to million-year-old frosts, the ghosts of forests.

We think we hear riders call to one another,
slap of rein against flank,
stamp of unshod hooves.
The air is too thin.
    We dream of axes.

Weeks of shifting stone then we discover
six guardian horses
grand in their gold-antlered headgear.
Melt the milky ice to find her last meal: mutton.
    Then open the halves of her larch coffin.

Look at this human thing
of tattooed thumbs. The flowering tree of life.
Her body's cavities tamped with peat and bark,
with coriander, star anise and parsley seed,
    the furs of small animals.

In extreme old age they choose a new place each night,
their snow queen's train of sheets and quilts behind them.
She discovers the under-surfaces of things – the dining table, basin –
do not worry her. He wraps her in the crook of his arm.
One night, full moon in their conservatory, ice flocks along the cracks,
makes every breath she takes a gasp. Under whispery coats
they wear their last winter. She considers
all it has taken for *home*
to become four pockets, two hoods.
Stars rush at the glass roof, old galaxies
fall away from blue to grey to white furs, drifting.

Beatitudes of Love

from the painting by Stanley Spencer

The air is hungry, the dance hall hungrier.
Tip-tilted, bosomy, the women cut in
on the soapy, rumpled, meandering men,
squash and swag and feast on them
so wide-eyed as fish surprised they leap
tasting one perfect instant before the barb.

Mouth kissy-kinked inside his ear, her
musty *eau de foxfur* makes him blush;
so too the mulberry velveteen above
that's squirmed up in his fists, the knowing
there's boned peach satin down below;
most of all her scalloped gusset:

O! The great bleb, warpy, crinkled, seething, of her,
bunions and all, the warm, loose ringlets of her stockings,
all of her before him and beside him, a gamey continent
he's spent his man's life bouncing in as if she were
deep and double-sprung, endless and echoless,
and will again in the moss-dark quietus of tonight!

Spindly, big-stiff beau in suiting better fitted to his father,
she'd rather have him, slanty-shouldered, bandy,
than any Errol Flynn, let anybody argue. She sees
pollen smudges round him,
a shirred paradisal glaze that makes her lick
her lips – she knows the angels that have always lived
loll around them now, tease their last-gasp flame to glory.

Away

In my forty-ninth year the old house turned its face away,
forbidding me to enter even in dreams.

Smell of the sea and Brasso, the barometer
stuck on 'changeable' and the front gate sticking,

stone cobbles still waxy with rain
in that Pends doorway we always ran through

circling like Sufis against the wanton spirits wanting us
to slip and strip the skin from our blue knees:

I could fly over the castle and Queen Mary's tree,
watch the lights coming on in Market Street

but the window where I used to see the banisters
glisten, the lowered head of my father, dense and dark,

the glass roof-well that pounded with storms,
my L-shaped poltergeist's attic

and the long, combed fields of the Largo Road
streaming away from my head stuck out of the skylight,

all shut like a Thursday early closing with grey haar
vanishing it slant, if you looked away.

Mama Yew

You squat lopsided in my churchyard
showing your dirty knees between petticoats
shagreenish, slept-in, prinked with star-burns.
Around you the children run.
Dorothy Ann, Died 2 Years And 10 Months.
Martha, Died Aged 5 And ½ Years.
Catherine Jane Who Died Feby. 9th 1873
Aged 7 Months.
You are hiding in plain sight
but O, the terror of never being found!
I was a child
running in this garden.
Remember the Caithness mason, feeling for a fault
in the grain, saying
some stones can break your heart?
I do not think the dead approve of you,
abandoning suitcase after suitcase,
smaller and smaller shoes:
Come out, come out, you cry, *the moon is shining*
bright as day! But you are a fist of shadows,
all-bearing, all-hollow,
you will not allow –
you pull me
in again, ring-a-ring of roses,
I let the dark
smudge you across the glass
into my own face.
I'll shut the door
and live with myself,
my Whitby jet, my blackbird's wing,
my washed-up sea coal.
I'll crawl in
under your spikes.

Acrobat

after Chagall

When Otto played, moonlight
spilled from his violin

your sister ran from shade to shade
worried you would be left behind
in the forlorn apartments

but Ezekiel whispered in your right ear
and dusted with immortality
you flew on

into the wall of light

Our Lady of the Snows

Prague

Midwinter dusk
thickens in our throats.
Not lost but
not knowing this square,
we are crossing its lit frames
leaving no shadow.

And then aware of snow
touching us and falling away,
we seek shelter in her cave of velvets
as she flies above her city
relinquishing her children,
her thin and chilly flames

luminous seedlings
made human
just at the moment of their vanishing.

In the City of the Headless Overcoat

Night falls away to morning's bruising of vermilion.
We cover the burning ash with lime
and so the river promises: I shall be obsidian.

Within the paper-thin pavilion
wedding tables bleach with early rime.
Night falls away to morning's bruising of vermilion.

A neighbourhood consigned to silvery oblivion
by spiders who write/rewrite the sorrows of our kind.
And so the river promises: I shall be obsidian.

Nailed up at every door, the shoes of our dead children.
From silenced stairs and courtyards left behind,
night falls away to morning's bruising of vermilion.

Come now, the ghost battalion,
faces white with gas, lips hooked on fishing line.
And so the river promises: I shall be obsidian.

This dog star time's claimed its dominion:
you who sang are mute, who saw are blind.
Night falls away to morning's bruising of vermilion
and so the river promises: I shall be obsidian.

The Karlovy Vary Trains

16.12.2008

for Mike Lauermann and Kiss Árpád

By chance on this day, in this city, in this nearly-used-up year,
we walk snow sheets of intersections,
scrawls of the living and dead,
silver peeling back from the dark of the glass.
A step is a word. A word in a known or unknowable language
speaks and is heard, presses down, lifts itself free
then of its own volition presses down again
in another place. Each step a word, and no matter
how erased, defaced, a witness.

Praha Hlavní Nadraží

Under domed space, in a kind of wide-eyed sleeping,
travellers bundle together, hobbled pigeons
stunned by cold and stunted by an emperor's ballroom
over whom nymphs soar,
blinded, bare-breasted – and as if from some after-life,
muttering *Co si pamatuješ? What do you remember?*
Slow trains wash in, so rails shine with almost invisible snail-ink
then blur to whispers in white air.

Masaryk

Moving wall, uniform, all slanted visors
and boots laced to the shin, police swarm the concourse
short-cutting to a fascist march
on the street outside. Its marching step, unseen,
voiceless, only a *thud thud thud* on the edge of hearing,
like detonations of small, very far away explosions.
No faces turn.
That stamp-echo, its dumb space,
stays long after their vanishing.
I rip a poster through its four black hooks,

31

turn and see more pasted
in postal rows on the wall's grey envelope.
Hate Hate Hate
These are my words. These are not my words.

Crypt of the Church of Saints Cyril and Methodius

Blunt nubbed bullet holes. A strait stair
down into the dark, stone hive
where they lay to the final day, death with its heart still beating.
Far to the east, windowless trains are running
on sleepers muffled with leaf-fall enamelled in snow,
a chalk scrawl on a sliding door. The map
of a boot print across a face.
The holes are big enough to fit my thumb.
How many more dead than living travel with us
when we go on.

Malátová

This viscous river shape-shifts
behind my back till I spin round, then is white as an eye.
Cobbles slide underfoot like fists, like noses.
Dust-felted in a junk shop window, torsos of Hussars, imperial
tureens,
iridescent spoons, war medals, crucifixes, hide in plain sight
and knocked-about, homely, a horse on exhausted strings –
not asking to be loved again, long beyond all that,
but I would offer anything, the rest of my life,
this moment now, to ride him blue as bone
through the knots and mazes of this city, his echo
of sparks in neon twilight proof
none of this imagined me. Snow clots again
into cracks and corners, shadows ahead
seem more present than their bodies
and I remember him already, a stream running clear
as he leaps in his fine coat of flame, hooves flecked with stars.

Strašnice

Smoky evening. I bring a stone
to this stony place, rest it on the sill of one grave.
A face seems to push through to surface, blind,
in a slip of the light.
I think of you, searching the long rows from number-post to
                                                  number-post
for all the family you lost, gaps
in the shadowland of home.

Staroměstska

We circle back to where grey, aged children
in weighty coats with a 1940s cut
observe the deceiving hour between snakeskin and velvet:
sparks fly up, knit into nuclei, splutter to earth again,
bleach through skin, bone, wool: the city is stippled with glitter
and Christmas. Death swings his tinkly bell
to a flurry of camera flash, small-talk of café pianos.
I am not moving through this city, it is travelling me.
From high drones, aerial shots of trains
are being taken, breathing low and insistent
as sea-memory in this landlocked country.

Praha Hlavní Nadraží

In failing light a woman sweeps the empty halls
of smudges our morning footprints made.
We waited for you, Árpád, in Wenceslas Square,
knowing you weren't coming as yourself
but as your long-haired, 1974 photograph.
And if you came, then we looked right though you,
like sleepwalkers meeting.
Illusion-memory, the prickling of our skins
when we came through by grimy photograph
their bodies on the pavement,
soles of their shoes exposed –

Out along the platform, dimly, a reel
of carriage windows unroll, click, click, click,
each frame a still of stories being forgotten, but together,
small houses lit against the dark.
Silence, then salt and pepper plash of snow,
curling lightly as feathers at our burning faces,
and Karlovy Vary trains, glowing, acid-daubed
Cyrillic, Slavonic, Hebrew, Hip-Hop,
are still departing hourly with soft exhalations of breath.

Overwintering

A green bareness, masculine, cold, murmurs in the bedroom,
camphor and hair oil on the unslept-in sheets.

Like living in Antarctica and leaving no footprints,
climbing the unlit stairs night after night for half a childhood

the house undoes you
in such a way it comes looking, years later,

sea air testing the loose frames
to find some way in.

Dog Hour

Where is the world?
Seeped away
whole:

violet, lost, a deep sea
phosphorescence of
disembodied voices

calling up forms
who running, swimming, flying
cannot answer:

lamps come on across the park
incoming planes
soundless but starry

The Captain Plays Shostakovitch on an Upright Piano, Field Hospital, Helmand Province

Where his hands fall
a spring rises
cold and clear,
busy with sticklebacks

hissing of rocks split under fire,
moon-quarries, craters
studded with sandbags,

the dawn slit a slashed pink along the ridge
and Jo, skylined, going down – big Jo
who'd shouldered through an archway

filled in by boulders,
knocked a Jo-shaped hole
his whole platoon came stumbling through

clear and cold,
busy with sticklebacks
a spring is rising

Jo, you are whole and bare,
the perfect circle
a diver forms
on entering the water

Beijing Flight, Thursday Morning

for Jack

Your cream linen back making for the airport
heaving the suitcase with the broken lock

snatching the yellow ticket from the short-stay machine,
pick up/drop off/goodbye, driving with headlights dipped

through summer downpour, foggy hedges and lying-down cows,
talking about nothing, memories and jokes, dropping

one brother at his school gates, waving as he runs and
checking passport, shiny red Mao money one more time, blowing

a kiss to the other brother, shirtless at the door,
cramming the boot with luggage and the new straw hat

you're not sure about,
standing still in the hall, in a green cloud

of your father's fragrance, his voice on the phone from the London
train
warm and fuzzy, *safe journey* and *I love you*

tea and a bagel, a hot shower, waking
to early rain on your attic window

sleepwalking through the night with dreams of wandering
corridor after corridor –

we've done this before but I'm hopeless at goodbyes,
I let you through my hands, a smudge

of smoke, your cream linen back,
over and over again, from the beginning.

Passing Place

for Sam

On a hill road between buzzards,
masters of sky, and those stumblers,
pheasants, under our wheels,
between woods
braided with ancient trees, hedgerows,
and the Wild Beast of Cheviot slipping
gold-eyed in, we pause,
slowing right down
but still startling them, those two fine
bays, whose shoulders we look up to
as if at deities disguised
in deep sleep of days,
sharing our passing
then forgetting us.

nobody belongs here,
nothing to be owned
only the shared dome
of treetops, the shabby
threads in their weave of bark, trace
on the unswept floor that arrived
here years ago and stayed:

you don't question, you are too small, in this room
of gigantic skirting boards and overhanging velvets,
too temporary, you who can only pass through,
cannot know how the wind sounded then, or how it will keen
over your body when you are lain across the branches
and the trees fall again and the sorrel grows over them,
the mushrooms through them and the honey fungus writes

in elaborate scripts across their inner skins, a Sanskrit
or Arabic, a pattern only, and only beautiful.

Stella Maris

I sail a shipwrecked Tesco trolley
my hair's a thicket of herringbone, my boots
yawn with the blue, lolling tongues of long-drowned seamen
I rolled from the Tyne:

my coat's swaddled with stories, I contain *Suns*,
Worlds and *Times*.
Spells rattle their wheels along the quay,
all squeaky rosaries and rigmaroles:

ripped long ago by hooks
I mistook for stars,
no companion have I
but my ship's cat, *Imaginary*.

Frieston Shore

For the world ends here,
the old world, unclean.

For our men are held at the Stump,
bent to the wind like beasts,

their boat unbuilt.

For we are theirs, left
to serve and sever

with one swing each,
stride a dry sea of unboiled heads.

For flesh must eat.

If the blade slips inside my hand
blood cold and ungenerous must come.

For I have made pilgrimage
beyond mortal travelling,

stones under my tongue.

It belongs not to my care
whether I die or live here,

for I bend my back, I gouge
cuts in the land, channels:

turn not Thy face from us

for this scourged firmament of want
and changeable shore

is the new world's skin,
softest about the scar.

Tide Turn

Slam and bang of unbending hammers,
unbelonging cranes, anxious to be away,
their boom and murmur.

Bolted together, river, bridge, river,
bred and born. Slow coagulating
oils gild brick embankments,

white cliffs of wharf and spill of gullwings'
undersides, a flash of nacre.
Quick and quiet, the turn of tide,

sky draining light from electric water,
hackles high, a jolt of fur-brushed static.
Joined, enjoined, traffics

of ship or spar, oyster shell, coinage
from Rome and Romanies, brick dusts,
human hair and hagstones

will nose-dive north,
north-west, while inlaid into carrion
membrane, the bridge's

whale jaw or elephant's backbone
teems with beads and droplets, popping,
high above the sailors' bethel.

Black-hearted staithes
that suck last breaths of suicides or call
of seabirds, cyclical:

leatherwrack belt, keeping the river lean.
And somewhere in between,
lent, the gap where the ships were.

Night-Flying Bees

From a westerly wind and the tall square-rigger *Manitou*
(moored in the bay en route for Tahiti)
a curious thing squeezes out of the medicine chest
left with its lid ajar by a love-sick, disjaskit captain
and lifts in the violet air, tasting this northern hemisphere,

spiralling for pure pleasure through this night of nights
scented with brine and silverlings and sea lavender
before, bored with the same old rum-snoring sailors,
going off to search for its own kind,
to breeze through an East Wynd casement,

curling in with the night air, sweet-brewed,
so Elspeth Deuchar's mouth falls open by an inch,
she's dancing flamenco in a cramasie-bodiced dress
for a ballroom of unicorns; her carriage idles
ready to sweep her over the hills. Her lips

feel slippery as honey. She rubs her toes
along her lover's instep: he purrs in his sleep
halfway across the Grand Canyon on a high wire,
hands waving swords of yellow gladioli –
while Sarah Scourie's sweater, knitted with sore bent fingers,

unrolls, a blue-grey sea of syllables, row after row
wave upon wave, the true story of her long life.
And Fiona's stubborn bread dough, knuckled under, laughs and is
                                                        a baby.
And stump-legged Sandie roars on the rise and swoop of a force ten,
white walls slamming the deck, breath torn out of his ribcage,

his red hair on end in pointy arrows, yelling
Montevideo! Tierra del Fuego! Lower Largo! And each
time the swell yoiks him up like the best joke he's ever heard.
And the minister's wife finds the whale tooth lost in that fire,
holds it in her hands again, smoothes over her father's scrimshaw
                                                        lullaby

out of the strong came forth sweetness, then puts it to her mouth.
And Jamie's long-gone mother whispers *hushie-ba, hushie-ba,*
wheesht now
as he leaps like a dog into the soap and soda shallows of her lap.
At first light the *Manitou* sails, leaving no sound or trace
in the milky water; and clustering around the proud

bare-breasted lady where she commands the prow, nuzzling
those salt-polished pointy hives, there's an odd, airborne smudge
of those
surprised to wake and find themselves so far from gorse and heather
and seaswept
gardens, from their own beds: light-headed a little, even dizzy, from
so much sweet feasting out of sorrow.

Four Poems, Shepherds Dene

Bonfire Site

I am soft ash; unsqueamish slate.
Old I am, somewhere, suasive, dark,
but slip veils suavely as a snake
and seem, green-strewn with meadow-grass,

scabious and vetch, disguised from you who pass.
I'm stroked by shadows; high trees shake
windblown cones upon me. I'm a craft
strange and changeable, becalmed upon a lake.

Thus far have I acquiesced; but ached.
Sprawled wide then dwindled to a boot-kicked mark,
bruise of good riddance in its unlovely place,
still may I, slyly, couple once more with the spark.

I breathe, I last.
Only the broken cannot break.

Rusty

is a no-nonsense, all-weather brown,
sports a joyful red wheel bow tie.
Upside down, back-to-front against a shed, he
kicks back, relaxes. Has no decisions to take.
Like a labrador, prefers to be firmly but fairly treated,
enjoys solidarity with stone in shade.
Has something of the bull about his handles,
is a subject for poetry.
It's enough.
He's never wanted to dance.

Trough with Lichens

Maiden-ladylike,
grey bonneted,

tappy-lappy and
shower tabbied,

dew pearl-pricks
on shabby tippet fur,

all polka dot corsage, silvery-
liverish, oystery

eau-de-nil –
Aspicilia, Candelariella, Parmelia,

Côte d'Azur imaginings
(for a sprightly stay-at-home)

of cancan swirls at ankle,
underwings scumbled in gold.

Range

You could have followed a Roman army by ear.
An hour to trudge unseen behind the forest, another two or three
to the ridge, days apportioned from a thousand steps.

Not so the fighter jets: their noise never catches up. Gone
before they appear, a rip in the soft blue world,
and on Otterburn range gunfire slams, echo first.

The sole of a foot fits itself around, allows for, remembers
the life it has known, the land it has touched, as sky
dilates and absorbs, does not forget.

Seacoaling

A January man scrapes the sea for coal,
hauls it from its froth still
shining –
soft necklaces of jet, strands
of a Gypsy woman's hair
scribbled across the shallows.

Shirtless, smoking, he lugs
bucket after bucket
the long stagger to the dunes
and his bored mare, strapped to her cart,
grinding sea grass down between
bone-yellow gums.

An easterly rips in across his shoulder blades,
so flesh, wishy-washy round a florid heart
and indigo anchor, cringes –
like teeth marks, the coal-bits mottle
his forearms and chest to a samurai armour
or Steptoe overcoat.

More and more now he thinks he hears them
from the undersea shaft, long unworked,
their tappings and callings: no fathers
or grandfathers of his.
Poor leavings, these,
that keep a needy fire alive.

Clown Wife

Solly, this life will be the death of us.
Fat man pratfalling,
each laugh hurts like a punch
for my poodle-man in a flimsy ruff.
Otto says he no longer finds you funny,
walks you like a tiger he has broken
and taken pleasure breaking.

I'll hold your heart up to all of them,
heavy glass jar of thick, bright honey,
show how it curls in its hot descent.
Solly, the boatman's waiting to carry us away.
Let it be tonight you vanish inside that costume,
its empty cloud collapsing on the stage,
an iron lung you won't need where we are going.

Mrs Greathead's Garden

An east wind is a sorry thing.

There's worse, he says.
The underworld.
Whinn Pitt, Endeavour.

But I, too, kneel, I bruise
alone:

there's turnips to rock back and forth out of their stubbornness,
tetties musty-scented as a bairn's scalp and rough but,
snagging on my thumbs,
a tousie heap among the straw,

rhubarb leaves ample as my best tureen
shade for the cat where he creeps in to sleep,
beans bowing their red blooms
as if sounding out trumpets:

other days
rain squall scudders in from the sea
salt grit in it to rive stalk from root,
scour cheeks red raw.

We'll not get the better of each other
yet –

yet my foot soles forget
hard-turned ridges of the earth I've dug
for further down the toom
suck of the dark.

Spelks of coal, blue
in my man's skin when he comes home
grow and curl like a vine,
like a thraw
in the vein.

The Seaweed Chandelier

Tides clean it mostly, and candlelight.
Washerwomen's tears and sailors' spit.
The heat and the cold.

How old is it?
It will not tell.
Old as today.

Chafing the silvered tarnish of the sea
into fantastical reflections
of lost eyes, eels,

it spatters with snowflakes'
see-through stars
burning gently to the bone

so ash of us, filigree,
lilts up as we dance beneath,
those of us who have nowhere to go
but the rest of our lives.

My Roseangle Bandstand

for Bob

We played pretend that dusk they left the deckchairs out,
musical chairs without music, then stood at the rail waving
as if from some liner coming into New York
and a man fishing on the Tay waved back.

Later I kissed you behind the ear,
years later, tasted early summer awnings
ivory and violet, greenwooded Balgay Hill, walled
gardens, north light soft as digestive biscuit

or black pepper coarsely ground,
cloud mountain coffee, damp woodsmoke burr
fossilised chocolate from your waistcoat pocket,
fox on a dustbin fossick,

streets and pavements starting to breathe
after the first hot day –
and the bandstand spinning in space, alone,
a moon in a misty hat.

There will be liquorice fume to both insides
of his desert boots, a blood-red
blood-warm row of beads at his dark throat,
rosemary rubbed through his blue jay hair,

the may, burning white now as the musty elder
instead of words, when I remember him.

Simrishamn

Big as a steamroller, grandiose and slow,
oblivious to hedgerow or wall
he comes through white dawn
to my garden at Simrishamn.

Dawn is his time – and mine:
I know he would have the smell of the woods on him,
their deep cold, as if in some dream
I had touched him, and remembered.

Mesmerised by roses
he nuzzles their icicle whites, their damasks
heavy-petticoated for this cold coast;
I can almost feel

their fondant snag his woolly tongue,
in his unhurried chew
melt to ambrosia, salt-sweet,
and lick my lips for happiness,

begrudge him nothing,
even the splayed-leg largesse
that leaves a sepia corsage upon my lawn:
only when he is entirely gone

do I taste his breath,
like the coming of snow
on the wind from the west, from the south,
winter, but with roses in it, somewhere.

Fever Walk

for Theo

How we fought to get you born, how you fought back!
My foot-shaped bruises on the midwife's hip,

finally, boxers mangled from a frenzied bout,
for our own good, they separate us –

rush you away.

Through these hours I walk you
in my arms, light as a dropped bird,

all hollow bone and eggshell skull,
I walk through doors falling open over and over,

heavy-headed roses:

each step a stronger echo till the dark,
worn fine, begins to craze and marrow-juice pours out,

the stuff of mornings, lifetimes,
thick and salty cry:

you open your mouth wide.

Elspeth Owen's bowl

is hand-formed from a coarse clay body
then burnished to pale ochre-green and cobalt's
soft greys, given a low firing
with shards, salt and seaweed;

some controlled cooling to assist the growth of crystals,
then glazes, poured, allowed to overlap.
Iron endows rich mustard, copper, moorland greens,
turquoise blues and oxbloods

burnished first at leather-hard stage then later, again,
with the back of a spoon. Now the whisper of your fingers
accepts from me this craft that will carry you away,
precious ship whose cargo and soul are one and the same –

feldspar, dolomite, bone, ash.

Newala

Letter from my son

He saw the fever tree first,
forty years higher than in my photograph,
then the house, red-roofed,
low built against the heat,
its white veranda
as if untouched –
and the plains below
clear to the Mozambique border.
Close up, he saw those steps
gap-toothed, crumbling.
Wrote: *something shivered and crept in me.*

In the rainy season of the fourth year of my life
I would lie under that roof, heart's yammer
a spoon knocking in a tin bowl,
a man beating a dog.
Door opening into the dark over an invisible drop
I would look at water poured into my glass,
listen to ghosts drinking.

The photograph brought him here
to my father in his straw hat,
the dogs slumped in the cool
beside the wall: my mother, stunned by the sun.
Something shivers and creeps in me.

Now I am walking the path towards the steps.
Look, I say, pulling him forward,
welcome us. I raise my hands.
Your unexpected guests.

Hope

Hope is winter light –
its wordless drench on skin.

Is a button from the button tin
cloudless tone just right
for the coat you're walking in –

hope is a three-toed signal in the snow,
a bird paused here,
that's all you know –

hope is a pocket-stone forgotten long ago
found by your hand and known
as a corm is married to the loam:

is day arriving, numb and slow.
Hope is a coat, that's all.

You pace the cracks, each step
a whisper: *don't let go*
while, catching up behind, that echo,
letting go, *letting go*.

Spending One Day with Patrick Kavanagh

I took the train from Cork that day
to quell the chewing voice that said
I have to go and see that man before I'm dead.

Dublin's air was oyster grey, the river like an unmade bed.
Between us we had what we had to say.
A gull sat a while upon his head.
Though it turned chill I had to stay,
the two of us unwashed, unfed.

And no one ever knew that way the years of speechlessness I shed.

Coalend Hill Farm 1962

I don't remember the Beanley orra-man,
his boots down the lonnen black as a wet day, his caravan
under a butchered elm's imaginary wingspan,
rusted, cantankerous: *all that can's been done*,
my mother said, then, low, *he's God's own one*.
I can't recall his singing of the Kingdom come,
or whispering from underneath his hands
if my soul the Lord should take, or how he crept away
like Billy Blin, awake long hours before the blackbirds, eager to begin
carving off a dead lamb's skin to roll one barely living in
under a dazed ewe, force tongue to tit, tit to tongue:
mole-blind he'd move, from east to western sun, more whole
in his Gomorrah than the doucest thing, but slow,
immortal, helpless as his beasts to conjure up tomorrow.

Leaving the Far Point

A bright, windy Dublin Sunday. Clouds and air and light attend, all tattered up together, swirling after-taste of sea or fore-taste of showers, snap of fresh linen, scenty tea for later: fill it in, Jack, with your invisible colours.

Jack, Cottie and Uncle walk on the shore, arm in arm, going at some speed for the wind's behind them. One's dead, one's living, and Cottie will be dead in two months: they are Easter yellows all, cherry blossom, spray curled waves, alive alive-o, and laughing, laughing.

How to remember it so it stays for ever, doesn't fade, doesn't blaze. Don't make it a postcard, don't colour the edges in, seal and shade. You don't know what it is you know; look slant, you'll see it. Like stars in a fathomless sky that only appear as you look away.

Jack is walking with the two souls he loves most in this world and all the others. In and out, and in between, all crack and bluster, it doesn't matter now. Colour the memories in, change them around, let them go, wash them away, let them rise, circling, a smear of blues and greys that dissolve and fall and spiral up again in the shake of a brush.

I am walking through and among a surge that twists and snarls at the Grafton Street traffic lights, blur of see-through and opaque faces, some living, some ghosts, some dragged back by us and some alone, nearing their time, and I can't tell, when I look fleetingly into the tide, when I make space between oncoming bodies which touch and do not touch, which is which.

Except that like Jack and Cottie and Uncle they are, and I am, transparent, lucid, simple and perpetual as water.

And it occurs to me: I don't have to lay you away, wrap you and keep you anymore; you're tired of my haunting you, dragging you along, you never wanted to be my shadows. You'd rather be walking to the far point, arm in arm, blown-about and laughing, laughing, alive, alive-o.

Notes

p. 9 *Solstice* 'dog or wolf': 'L'heure entre chien et loup' is a French expression for dusk.

p. 14 *Cairn* In his book *Passage* (Thames & Hudson, 2004) Andy Goldsworthy writes of building Penpont Cairn on the crest of a small hill above his Dumfriesshire village. 'Cairn' is a found poem in which all the words have been taken from that account.

p. 16 *Home News* All the words are from one edition of the local weekly paper the *St Andrews Citizen*.

p. 22 *Dew Point* The temperature to which air must be cooled for water vapour to condense to dew. When the dew-point temperature falls below freezing, the water vapour creates frost or hoarfrost.

p. 23 *The Flowering* In 1993 the Russian archaeologist Natalya Polosmak discovered the mummified body of a 2400-year-old woman buried in the permafrost of the Ukok Plateau in the Altai Mountains. Because of her extensive, beautiful tattoos, it is believed that she was a powerful shaman or storyteller.

p. 26 *Away* The Pends is a mid fourteenth-century stone gatehouse of the Augustinian cathedral priory of St Andrews.

p. 29 *Our Lady of the Snows* Kostel Panny Marie Sněžné, once intended to be the grandest church in Prague. Only the chancel was completed, but its dark Baroque makes an overwhelming opposite to snows outside.

p. 30 *In the City of the Headless Overcoat* A statue in Prague's Jewish Quarter honours Franz Kafka. It shows an empty coat with a small man on its shoulder.

pp. 31–4 *The Karlovy Vary Trains* A circular walk around Prague on one day in December 2008. It begins and ends in the main railway station, Praha Hlavní Nadraží. The underground level is modern but above ground the Art Nouveau stained glass, statuary and marble are half-abandoned in their grandeur.

Crypt of the Church of Saints Cyril and Methodius The Orthodox Church of Carlo Borromeo, dedicated to St Cyril and St Methodius, hid a group including two British-trained Czech agents, Jan Kubiš and Jozef Gabčik, after their assassination on 27 May 1942 of Reinhard Heydrich, the German SS leader and chief planner of the Final Solution. They were sheltered in the crypt, sleeping in empty coffin-bearing niches in the wall, until they were betrayed by a fellow-agent, Karel Čurda. As the church was overrun on

18 June some were shot and others chose suicide over capture. Terrible reprisals followed Heydrich's death.

Strašnice   The 'new' Jewish cemetery, opened in 1891, less well known than that in the Old Town. Large gaps never to be filled with graves show how many descendants of Jewish families have been lost.

p. 42   *Frieston Shore*   A hamlet in Lincolnshire, once on the coast and popular in Victorian times for sea-bathing, but now a mile or so inland among saltmarsh and wetland due to coastal change. A Puritan community, the Scroop Brethren, lived here: some were imprisoned at Boston Stump (St Botolph's Church) for their beliefs. Following a failed attempt to sail to Holland to settle there, they sailed to America with the Founding Fathers and helped to set up the 'new' Boston.

p. 44   *Night-Flying Bees*   Some folk tales refer to dreams as 'night-flying bees'.

p. 48   *Seacoaling*   The 'black beaches' of Lynemouth in Northumberland have seen generations of both Travellers and local people making a precarious living from collecting waste coal that has been washed ashore.

p. 50   *Mrs Greathead's Garden*   A sketch map dated 20 March 1755 from Northumberland County Archives shows boreholes and mining activity in Black Close Colliery (now Cambois), including 'Endeavour Pitt' and 'Whinn Pitt' (*sic*) in the vicinity of 'Mrs Greathead's Garden'. 'Toom' means 'empty' and 'thraw' is to writhe or twist. It is also an old mining term for a fault in the rock.

p. 53   *Simrishamn*   A short piece in the *Guardian* described how elks invaded gardens in the town of Simrishamn, south-west Sweden, to eat the roses.

p. 55   *Elspeth Owen's bowl*   I found a description and image of Elspeth Owen's bowl in *The Potter's Palette* by Christine Constant and Steve Ogden (Chilton Book Company, 1996).

p. 57   *Hope*   This takes as its starting-point Emily Dickinson's poem 254, 'Hope is the thing with feathers –'.

p. 58   *Spending One Day with Patrick Kavanagh*   From a BBC Radio 4 interview with Brendan Kennelly.

p. 59   *Coalend Hill Farm 1962*   An 'orra-man' is a farm labourer. 'Billy Blin' is a Border/Scots Lowlands household spirit.

p. 60   *Leaving The Far Point*   From a painting of the same title by Jack B. Yeats in the National Gallery of Ireland. Finished in 1946, it shows an imaginary meeting of the most beloved people in Yeats's life: his wife Cottie (who would die two months afterwards) and his uncle, already dead, walking together with Yeats himself at Rosses Point, County Sligo.